The Magic Hour

Vanessa Bates

CURRENT THEATRE SERIES

First published in 2024
by Currency Press Pty Ltd,
Gadigal Land, Suite 310, 46–56 Kippax Street, Surry Hills, NSW 2010, Australia
enquiries@currency.com.au
www.currency.com.au

in association with Lulu Bell Productions

Typeset by Brighton Gray for Currency Press.
Printed by Fineline Print + Copy Services, Revesby, NSW.
Cover shows Jan Hunt, Louise Chapman and Amy Vee; cover design by Steve Black.

Currency Press acknowledges the Traditional Owners of the Country on which we live and work. We pay our respects to all Aboriginal and Torres Strait Islander Elders, past and present.

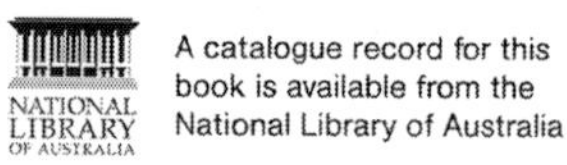

Contents

The Magic Hour was first presented by Upstage at the Playhouse and Lulu Bell Productions at Civic Theatre Playhouse, Awakabal and Worimi country, Newcastle, on 21 November 2024, with the following cast:

ACTOR 1	Jan Hunt
ACTOR 2	Louise Chapman
SINGER	Amy Vee

Playwright and Director, Vanessa Bates
Producer, Louise Chapman
Art Design, Steve Black
Composer and Sound Designer, Amy Vee
Additional Sound Design, Ross Mueller
Lighting Designer, Lyndon Buckley
Stage Manager, Kate Dun
Operator, Alana McGaughey
Technical Services Operator, Amanda Watt
Costume Designer, Kat Hood

PERFORMERS

ACTOR 1
ACTOR 2
SINGER

CHARACTERS

'Carla's Story'
CARLA
GRANDDAUGHTER

'Collette's Story'
COLLETTE
CINDERELLA

'Jeanette's Story'
JEANETTE
KING
PRINCESS
FROG
JOURNALIST

'Hannah's Story'
HANNAH
RAPUNZEL
YOUNG FATHER
YOUNG MAN

'Jane's Story'
JANE
SISTER
JACK
JACK'S DAD

This play text went to press before the end of rehearsals and may differ from the play as performed.

1. ONCE UPON A TIME

This 2024 life can seem a harsh one; a post-pandemic world with growing climate change, cost of living, wars, homelessness, fake news, mental instability, AI and social media consequences.

What is left for us to hope for in such a fearful, insecure, unbelievable world of not enough, too much and not again?

What is left to matter?

Well ... Love matters. Kindness matters. Caring matters. And Courage matters.

And because of all these things, or perhaps at the start of all these things ...

Stories matter.

The time: Twilight. With lots of noise—perhaps railway station and shopping centre and main street all mixed up together.

And threaded through this world, we hear some of the sounds of the fairytale world—the howl of wolves, the North Wind, the chorus of frogs, the creak of carriage wheels, bells ringing, doors slamming, leaves rustling, glass smashing ...

The place: Under a freeway? By a forest? In a corner of a huge city rail station?

On a blasted heath or a forgotten alleyway?

We are there, yes, but also, in a place where travellers might gather. For company. For stories. Here, there may be discards from society; human, rubbish, junk, rotting tree stumps and rusting oil drums, old clothes and holey shoes. And creeping, here and there, signs of life. Vines curled around iron bars, leaves shooting up amidst tin cans and discarded tyres. Nature, fighting to take back what was once hers.

The SINGER *appears, making her way onstage between the large garbage bins. She seems weary, drinks from her can. She has a guitar slung over her shoulder, a keyboard set up onstage, a milk-crate chair. A corner to rest.*

She hums to herself, plays some notes. She has the final sips out of her can. Pauses as she looks around. Which bin? She casually walks to the closest and drops the can in before returning to her spot.

Nearby the piles of clothes and rubbish begin to writhe and move. ACTOR 1 *emerges and makes her way slyly to the bin. The lid of the bin is suddenly flung open and* ACTOR 2 *emerges triumphant with the can. The* SINGER *watches them both, bemused.*

ACTOR 1 *hurrumphs and moves towards a makeshift stove. Stirs at a saucepan, tastes the results.*

ACTOR 1: [*ad-libs a bit, making sure audience is in place*] Come on you lot. Sit yourself down. Always room for the weary traveller. Like this one here. [*gestures at the* SINGER] You comfy, love? That's good.

Claim your spot. Grab your seat. Join in, find your place!
I got mine. Right here. You like?

Indicates the stage.

Food, shelter, wifi … all the basics.

Chuckles.

Get those right, nice and tight, and I can share with you something special.

ACTOR 2 *climbs out of the bins, collects cans and checks other bins.*

ACTOR 1 *looks around.*

Nearly time.

She waves the ladle at them.

I'm having soup. Smell good? Start with a stone. Know that story? 'Stone Soup'?

Family recipe, handed down
got it from *my* mother.
She got it from hers.
And *she* got it from Jamie Oliver's next-door neighbour's grandma!

Nah. Just a joke.

Turns to the SINGER.

What about you? Singing's hungry work, isn't it? Feel like some soup? Won't be long.

Tastes it.

Needs something … ooh I know.
Little bit of thyme …

ACTOR 2 *picks some from a pot, offers it.*

ACTOR 2: Time … just a pinch.
ACTOR 1: That's all we need. Might even have time … for a story?

The SINGER *starts to play her guitar.*

SINGER: Once
upon a time …
in a democracy, in a country, in a colonial outpost far far away.
On the fringes …
on the margins, on the edges of the nation …
On an island …
in a city, by a dark dark forest …

Music. And as she speaks we have a sense that the world around her is changing, just a little. Because we're listening.

ACTOR 1: Cars still rushing, traffic crushing.
Crowds stop working, shadows lurking …
SINGER: The Magic Hour
Sunset hour
Half dark, half light, half black, half white.

Music.

ACTOR 1: Creeping, croaking, hurry home and get your tea, mum's waiting, dog's barking hour.
Last run at backyard cricket, last jump at elastics, last bit of telly hour …
[*As* MUM] *Turn that bloody thing off and come and have your dinner.*
ACTOR 2: [*as* KID] *Not yet, Mum!*

Music.

SINGER: Magic hour, sunset hour, nearly time for story hour.

ACTOR 1: [*as* MUM] *If I count to three, you'll get a thick ear ... One, two ...*

ACTOR 2: [*as* KID] *Coming, Mum!*

SINGER: Falling hour, squalling hour, heads down and drooping hour.

Music.

ACTOR 1: Almost sleeping, eyes still peeping.
Dinner hour, bath hour, brush teeth and bed hour.

ACTOR 2: And are we ready?

SINGER: And are we ready?

ACTOR 1: And are we ready?

Pause.

Then we'll begin.

2. CARLA'S STORY

The SINGER *and* ACTORS *howl together.*

ACTOR 1: Hear something? Feeling nervous? It's alright. We're safe here.

Beat.

Maybe.

There's a story you might remember. Bit scary. Bit nasty.

SINGER: A little girl in red?

ACTOR 2: And a big bad wolf?

ACTOR 1: What's that you say? 'Little Red Riding Hood'?
Nup.

This is Carla's story.

Lights transition. ACTOR 2 *becomes* CARLA.

ACTOR 2/CARLA: My granddaughter's missing again.

She hands out some flyers. Stops to examine one.

Done these at Officeworks. 'Have you seen this girl?' School photo. She doesn't usually look like that.

You seen her?

She wears this red cape thing, hoodie.
funny old thing she found in an opshop,
red boots and a miniskirt that barely covers her fanny.

Oh yeah. She's a right little tart.

Her mum turfed her out last year.

ACTOR 1 *becomes her* GRANDDAUGHTER.

Sick of all the blokes she was bringing home. She'd go out, used to say she was coming to see me, can you believe the cheek?

ACTOR 1/GRANDDAUGHTER: *Wanna see Grandma ... take her some treats, make her a cuppa tea.*

ACTOR 2/CARLA: [*with a wry smile*] Cuppa fuckin' tea. Can you believe it?

There she goes with her basket of leftover casserole or macaroni cheese
dumps it in the park
hangs out at the shopping mall or outside the pub, waiting for someone to give her a drink, cigarette
something.

There she goes getting picked up by the cops and brought home
her mother screams at her in front of them,
slaps her face, all that,
shows 'em:
[*As* MOTHER] *My kid's not allowed to get away with that sort of bullshit, officer.*

Next minute, kid's gone. Done a runner.

What do you do with a kid like that?

Sometimes I see her, coming home from the supermarket, or Bingo,
I see her, off her face, laughing:

ACTOR 1/GRANDDAUGHTER: *Hi Gran-Gran, hi Granny, hi Grand-ma-ma ...*
Whatcha get me? Something?

ACTOR 2/CARLA: I hate that,
'Gran'
sounds so old.

Not bloody old, I was eighteen when I had *her* mum, she was sixteen when she had her. Still got the figure, don't let myself get fat.

Look after my body.

Never know when you might need it. Eh?

It's this town that bends you, makes you old before your time.

Bloody staring eyes and all the whispering and crap that goes on. This place talks and it's not nice talk either—don't let that 'Best Tidy Town Three Years in a Row' bullshit you.

Nothing tidy about this place.

ACTOR 1: One road in and one road out.

Winters you freeze and summers you burn through the worn thin skin of the ozone layer.

Drive for hours through thick green forest on black ice bitumen. Trees grow flush against the side of the road.

Men died in these forests. Convicts. Ate each other and then got shot or flogged to death anyway.

ACTOR 2/CARLA: Not very fucking tidy if you ask me.

Makes you think—stop driving these roads, those trees'd take it all back. Roots bore through and up, crack back the grit and the tar …

And the road kill! You can run over animals you've only ever seen in zoos.

Things with spots and fangs and big black eyes.

There's real devils in there. Tigers too maybe.

ACTOR 1: But in this town,

all the animals walk on two legs.

ACTOR 2/CARLA: I came here with a man. Stayed for another. He told me he'd bash me if I left.

After a while someone ended up bashing him … by then I was stuck.

Got a house, not much but it's home.

Cold.

Goes right through your bones.

Feels like

you'd do anything to stay warm.

CARLA *looks at the photo on the leaflet.*

She came to live with me for a while.
It was alright. For a while.
Had her own room. Nice little white bed from Vinnies.
Bedside lamp I won at Bingo. Lots of little beads hanging down and there was this swirling sorta pattern on the sides. Forest.
Like in the old fairytales?
Yeah.
Trees and flowers and … a little path that wanders through. When you hit a switch the whole thing spins around real slow. Pretty. She liked it.

Sometimes at night I sit by her bed and she says:

ACTOR 1/GRANDDAUGHTER: *Tell me a story.*

ACTOR 2/CARLA: *Story? What kind of story? Can't remember any stories, love.*

ACTOR 1/GRANDDAUGHTER: *Tell me about when I was a baby.*

ACTOR 2/CARLA: 'Cause I had this thing see, I told her we all wanted her so much, a big star came down from the sky and we found her in a diamond cradle, all lit up by starlight and she was as small as my hand because she was a fairy baby, not a real human at all.

Fairy baby. She loved that.
And that was her story. Nice.

Although when she got bigger she'd say

ACTOR 1/GRANDDAUGHTER *and* ACTOR 2/CARLA: *Wish we'd kept the diamond cradle 'cause then we'd be fucking rich.*

They laugh together. Beat.

ACTOR 2/CARLA: After a while, she does her old trick.

Done a runner. Bought back a bloke. Told him he could stay.
He's a lot older than her. Tall bloke, skinny with long black hair.
Thought he might be one of those blow-ins, come over for the mines?
Blow-in. Fair enough. Aren't we all?
We all gotta start somewhere
Alright. He can stay. For a while.

She used to hang off him … giggle
play with his hair, get him tea and all that …

The noises they used to make.
Pair of animals.
Under my roof thanks very much.
Me sitting up on the lounge trying to watch *Masterchef.*

I didn't say anything. You never know with these men. They turn. That's my experience. Turn on a sixpence.
Eyes black as the night sky and wild, you know?
Dunno what a man like that'll do.

One time
sitting at the table in the kitchen, that little laminex one?
She's made dinner. Fish fingers. Veggies, mashed potato. She gets up to get something or other:

ACTOR 1/GRANDDAUGHTER: *Where's the tomato sauce?*

Beat. CARLA *is quiet, almost sly.*

ACTOR 2/CARLA: He pulls up his sleeves
shows me his tattoos.
Usual things, knife, skull, rose, but I can't help noticing
hair on his arms, under his sleeve, dark, strong hair.

He says: *Touch it.*

She reaches for him, hesitant.

Warm.

Beat.

One night, soon after that, he comes to my bedroom. Must have been with her earlier, I can smell that horrible perfume she wears, spray-on Impulse stuff, gets it from the chemist, like all the young girls. All the same.

See him at the door but I pretend to be asleep
then suddenly he's in my bed.
He's naked
I can feel that hair
all over his body
he strokes me
kisses me

he puts his mouth to my throat.

I don't scream.

When I bite into his lip our mouths fill with his blood.

I push him into me and I can hear the noises we're making, the growling and the yipping and the yelping and soon we're deep in each other's skins.

When we're finished, he falls asleep on my breast and I wrap the doona, warm, around us both

that's when I see her, standing by the bed.

She's just standing there. Staring.

Beat.

What big eyes you've got.

Bit hard for the kid. Find her boyfriend in bed with her gran.

She whispers as if her throat is full of crushed glass:

ACTOR 1/GRANDDAUGHTER: *He's mine.*

ACTOR 2/CARLA: *No.*

I'm careful not to wake him

He's my wolf now.

She makes a face, like … she's trying to smile.

And then she runs.

[*Calling after her*] *You'll be back!*

Pause. She examines the flyer, strokes the photograph. Regret.

The SINGER *plays gently, underscores.*

Course … she was a premmie baby.

Her mother was on speed and all the rest of it. Doctors just amazed the baby lived at all. Small as my hand. She was in that incubator for weeks and weeks.

Sometimes I'd sit by her and stroke her tiny arms and legs and she'd just shiver and cry, the tiniest thin little sound you ever heard.

I get up in the morning.

She's been back. Took her boots and her cape and some other things.

Took the lamp I won at Bingo. Don't know why. Can't use it where she's gone.

No electricity in the forest.

Music.

Swirling impression of the bedside lamp.

Music: *'Carla's Song'.*

SINGER: I know a path that leads through the dark
To you
I know a path that winds through the trees
To you
I don't need to see
The corpses you leave
To know I'd spill a little blood for you.

Lights change.

3. COLLETTE'S STORY

ACTOR 2, *rifling through the rubbish as* ACTOR 1 *stirs the soup.*

ACTOR 2 *finds one shoe, glittering, beautiful. Examines it. Holds it up to show* ACTOR 1 *and the* SINGER.

ACTOR 2: They say 'clothes maketh the man'.
I say 'shoes ruin the woman'. Or at least their feet.

ACTOR 1: Look at the height of that would you? Imagine getting around in those? Crazy! Wait, is there another one?

ACTOR 1 *grabs the shoe, imagines being three inches taller. Could be good.*

ACTOR 2: Nah.
Who'd be mad enough to wear a shoe like this?

Beat.

I think we all know the answer to that.
Take one fairy godmother, one pumpkin coach, one lovestruck prince and you get every little girl's fantasy …

ACTOR 1: … Cinderella. Right?

Beat.

But this is actually

Collette's story.

ACTOR 1 *places shoe down. Pumping techno music starts up.*

ACTOR 1 *becomes* COLLETTE.

COLLETTE *begins to dance, not entirely gracefully. She's self conscious and a little anxious, watching to see if anyone is watching her. Waves now and then at other dancers. We get the feeling they probably aren't waving back.*

ACTOR 1/COLLETTE: *Hi Tamara! Love your vampire cozzie! Hi James! Werewolf wig looks great!*

Music stops. She stares. In the background ACTOR 2 *becomes* CINDERELLA, *dancing.*

Oh. My. God.
That's her.
She's here.
[*To audience*] Yeah! Here, at the Virgins and Vampires Twilight Ball, even though my mum grounded her and everything.
And look what she's wearing!

Looks around checking others' reactions.

You should see my mum's face!
You should see *everyone's* face!
They're all like poking each other and pointing and whispering and you know what?

She doesn't even have an invitation!

She doesn't have an invitation, she doesn't have a pass or get her wrist stamped.
She rocks up in this gorgeous full-on goth carriage,
gives the door bitch the finger and walks right in!
Ohhh!

I'm dancing by myself near where my sister Olivia is dancing which is pretty near to where the prince and all his homies are hanging out
and I'm like: *Cinda! Cinderella! Wow you look so so ...*

Thinks.

Whatever that word is for you know, really really good!

But Mum's just like: 'Who forgot to deadlock the door?'

And she's like giving *me* the daggers, like she thought I forgot the deadlock, but it was so not me, it was Olivia.

She was all like … worrying about whether she looked fat in her dress or not and so she arks me and I'm like why are you arksking *me*? … you look fine, you look so whatever that word is for you know, really really good.

But you couldn't keep Cinda locked in anywhere she didn't want to be,

I mean she'd been in juvey, three months in detention, and she broke out that many times. If the bitch wanted to go ball,

the bitch would go ball,

you know what I'm saying?

Still watching CINDERELLA.

Mum tried to keep her occupied with some kind of pointless busy work—a basket of peas and a basket of dried beans all mixed up—told her she had till morning to separate the two but … as if!

Watching the scene play out in front of her.

Ohhh

It's like something out of a movie,

'cause Cinda just stalks up the aisle,

and she steps right up to the prince and she says:

ACTOR 2/CINDERELLA: *I hear this is your ball. Got another?*

COLLETTE *is shocked but loves it.*

ACTOR 1/COLLETTE: And he laughs!

He likes her.

And she looks like, totally hot, in that dress and those cool shimmy shoes she must have pinched from town because she never wears that gear round the house.

But … her real mum might have given it to her, better not start pointing the finger.

Oh sorry, when I say real mum? I actually mean 'fairy goddess mother'.

We call her Cornflakes.

She ran out when Cinda was a baby, joined some hippy commune.

Anyway, all this week, Cornflakes has been hanging around, burning incense and making rings of salt around the house.

Anyhow, now the prince and Cinda are dancing and they look so fully … whatever that word is for you know, really really good … and people are standing around clapping and calling out things like:

SINGER: *YO!*

ACTOR 1/COLLETTE: … and …

SINGER: *GET DOWN!*

ACTOR 1/COLLETTE: … and …

SINGER *and* ACTOR 1/COLLETTE: *THAT'S WHAT I'M TALKIN'* ABOUT*!!*

COLLETTE *waves at* CINDERELLA, *self-consciously, over the crowd.*

ACTOR 1/COLLETTE: *Cinda! Hi! It's me! Are you having fun?*

Points her out to the audience.

Man, I can't believe how amazing she looks. It's like her hair is full of tiny sparkly diamonds. Must be that new glitter spray. And her make-up. And her jewellery.

And the prince is so, totally, into her.

I wish someone'd look at me like that.

My dad used to say I was just a late bloomer.
One day I would change.
And I'd be perfect.
But he never said when that would happen.

Olivia's already left school.
Everyone says she's got beautiful skin.

Her hands move to her cheeks, self-consciously.

Mum says if I stop picking at my face, the spots'll go.

Sometimes I can't help it, you know? Like when I'm sort of imagining I'm beautiful and everyone loves me and I'm really popular and stuff, I find that I've been sticking my fingernails into my cheeks. Like this.

Except … really hard.

And kids rip me off about it. Call me Ackka-Dakka face and stuff like that. Dog woman. Fugly.

Freak.

Last week in Geometry I was thinking about that.

And then I felt … all wet. Lucky the seats were them plastic sort, like a little bucket.

But the girl across from me saw and she goes, really loud:

SINGER: *Oh no! Fugly's pissed her pants!*

ACTOR 2: And everyone kaks themselves and falls about laughing!

ACTOR 1/COLLETTE: And I go: *No, I haven't! I haven't! I must have sat in something wet.*

Slight pause.

And I wait till everyone's left the classroom and then I get up and I leave this pool of piss in my chair.

A clock chimes midnight. She stops, listens.

Midnight. Cool, this is so the latest I have ever been allowed out, you know?

Mum almost didn't let me go tonight. She *said* she was going to make me stay behind and sort out peas and beans with Cinda. I wish she had, 'cause then I would have come with *her* and I'd be giving the finger to the door bitch and dancing with the prince too.

It was 'cause of the wetting my pants and doing that thing to my cheeks and then she found out about the strips.

She looks at the audience, hadn't meant to let that out. Decides to take them into her confidence.

Oh … strips is what I call the little cuts I make on my legs.

She lifts her dress to reveal the bloodied lacerations.

Yeah. I've got like about fifty. I do 'em with this little knife that used to belong to my dad. It's real sharp.

They're so … straight. And neat. I make them exactly parallel. I cut them really slow so I can get them exactly right. And they are.

They're perfect.

In the background CINDERELLA *is having an argument.* COLLETTE *looks up.*

Ohhh! Cinda just chucked a spackatttack! She's like … pushed the prince out of the way and run up the hall!

CINDA *runs from the stage. Trips and shouts 'Fuck!' as she does.*

Ooh! She tripped over the cord to the DJ's booth. That must have hurt.

Nope. She's up. She's running. Gah. She even runs like a cool person. [*An idea*] I'm going with her!

[*Announces*] Everybody! Listen to me! This ball, is like … shithouse! I'm going too. I'm going with my sister Cinderella!

Cinda! Wait for me!

She tries to run after her, unsuccessfully.

She's gone. I thought … Maybe she had a taxi waiting or something. Is she walking home? 'Cause it's miles from here. I don't think I can walk that far.

Cinda! Wait for me! Cinda?

She looks around.

Someone's left a pumpkin lying on the step. That's not very safe. You could break your leg falling over a pumpkin like that.

She screams suddenly and darts out of the way.

Mice! That's disgusting. In a place like this? Hello, anyone heard of Rentokill?

Sees something on the ground—the shoe.

Ohhhhh!

Picks it up.

Must have come off when she was running …

[*Amazed*] Look how beautiful it is … perfect. Like her.

Ducks as she sees someone else coming out.

Ohh! The prince has come out to find Cinda. He's heartbroken! Look at him!

Excuse me!

She holds out the shoe to him, it's an impetuous offer but he takes it from her.

He's kissing it. Oh. My. God!

I wish I was that shoe.

Gasps.

He's using his tongue and everything. It's so … romantic!

It's slightly disgusting.

Maybe I should tell him I'm her sister. And where she lives … [*To Prince*] *Um ... excuse me. I know ...*

She stops suddenly, claps her hand over her mouth.

Whoa!

[*To audience, aghast*] He's saying he'll marry *the woman whose foot fits the shoe*!!

The prince has responded to her, she shakes her head in reply.

No, dunno. She must be a stranger round here. Sorry. Just wanted to say … good luck. Whoever fits that shoe will be a very very lucky girl.

May I?

She takes the slipper back, looks at it, wonderingly.

Such tiny perfect feet.

At the end of her skinny perfect legs.

On her skinny, gorgeous, perfect body with her beautiful gorgeous perfect head.

Music, underscoring.

[*Thinking*] I wouldn't have to cut off much.

A heel maybe … My big toe.

And if the shoe fits …

Just imagine it … My life would finally be … perfect.

Music: *'Collette's Song'.*

SINGER: Watch closely please
I'm crystal clear
In shoes of glass
I'm standing here

Keep watching me
I just might change

Peel back my skin
Unleash my rage

Music continues to underscore ... as we move into the next story ...

4. JEANETTE'S STORY

ACTOR 2: There's a big house, not far from here …
ACTOR 1: Big house. Beautiful house.
ACTOR 2: Fast car.
ACTOR 1: Lovely garden.
ACTOR 2: There's a woman.
You might have seen her. You might have met her.

Beat. A smile.

ACTOR 1: She might be you.

Music is outshouted by a chorus of frogs.

Those bloody frogs always start up when we tell this story!
ACTOR 2: Well, they would, wouldn't they?
They all know the story of 'The Frog Prince'.
But they don't know this version. [*To audience*] Neither do you.
ACTOR 1: Because … This is the story of Jeanette.

ACTORS *pull out out some puppets or even some stuffed toys and put them into position to mark the spot. A sad-looking doll sits at the centre. This is* JEANETTE.

[*Pointing them out*] So, here … The Queen. Jeanette.
Her husband, the King. Her daughter, Princess.
A buxom female reporter.
A photographer.
And … this all starts at dinner.
ACTOR 2: Tuna carpaccio for entrée. Very nice with a drizzle of olive oil.
ACTOR 1: Various roast meats for main. Cherry Ripe ice cream for dessert.
ACTOR 2: Table set beautifully. Rose-embroidered tablecloth. The one Jeanette's grandmother gave her.

Slight bitter pause.

For her dowry.

ACTOR 1 *picks up the* PRINCESS *doll and animates it.*

ACTOR 1/PRINCESS: *Mum! Dad! The people from the magazine are here! Taking pictures. Asking questions about what it's like to be us. Our family.*

ACTOR 2 *picks up the sad-looking* JEANETTE *doll and animates it.*

ACTOR 2/JEANETTE: We smile and we nod and my husband the king says to the journalist whose bouncing boobs are about to take off …

ACTOR 1 *picks up* KING.

ACTOR 1/KING: *Print this, darling! You do still print, dontcha? I want everyone to know, we're a normal, loving family!*

ACTOR 2/JEANETTE: And I'm sure that, tonight, we do sound like a … normal, loving family.

My *generous* husband. My *obedient* daughter.

He doesn't fart or slurp his wine or tell me how fat my arse has grown.

She doesn't scowl at me and say:

ACTOR 1/PRINCESS: *Mother! Why are we eating this shit?*

ACTOR 2/ JEANETTE: And me.

ACTOR 1: He used to call her his queen.

ACTOR 2/JEANETTE: Lately it's as if my teenage daughter can only see me when she scowls.

Unless she can peer through a filter of contempt and barely contained rage, it's as if I don't exist at all.

ACTOR 1: But tonight, she's on her best behaviour. Her daddy's promised an iPhone Fifteen.

Everyone sits and eats carefully, neatly.

And they look like a normal, loving family.

The camera whirrs and clicks around them.

And the journalist asks the daughter:

ACTOR 2/JOURNALIST: *What do you like to do for fun?*

ACTOR 1/PRINCESS *laughs.*

ACTOR 1/PRINCESS: *Actually, Daddy and I enjoy walks and playing in the courtyard.*

ACTOR 2: Her father heaves another half pig onto his plate and says …

ACTOR 1/KING: [*eating*] *Someone should tell her what I brought my little princess home from my last business trip. Nom nom nom.*

ACTOR 2/JEANETTE: For the Princess, a golden ball, beautiful item, thoughtfully chosen.

For me, his queen, another bout of chlamydia.

A noise.

What was that noise?

ACTOR 1: There's a noise just outside the dining-room door.

A … a splashing noise, like a garden gnome taking a bath in the hallway.

ACTOR 2: Everyone's silent … And then the knocking starts.

Sound of knocking. The FROG *appears, a puppet (or stuffed toy), from beneath the table.*

ACTOR 1: A voice, cold, clammy, not entirely unpleasant:

[*As* FROG] *Princess!*

A scream and a smash.

ACTOR 2: Princess screams, drops the olive oil … it smashes all over the imported Italian tiles.

ACTOR 1/FROG: *Open the door, Princess!*

ACTOR 2: Camera whirrs and clicks!

ACTOR 1/FROG: *Princess! How long must I wait?*

The journalist is gaping, open mouthed, scribbling away as if her acrylic fingernails were on fire. Who the hell's 'Princess'?

There's only one person at this table who gets called that …

Everyone turns to look.

ACTOR 2/JEANETTE: My daughter.

She sulks.

My husband raises an eyebrow at her. Gestures at the door.

She drags herself up with a lip you could serve dinner on.

Has a quick look, slams the door, runs back to the table.

ACTOR 1/KING: *Who is it at the door?*

ACTOR 2/PRINCESS: *Daddy … It's just a frog.*

ACTOR 1/KING: *A frog?!*

ACTOR 2/JEANETTE: He laughs and snorts and begins to splutter.

For a moment I think: my God, he's actually going to choke on that olive.

But instead, he clears his throat and the whole sodden mess flies through the room and sticks to my white damask curtains.

ACTOR 1/KING: *What does a* frog *want with you, Princess?*

ACTOR 2/JEANETTE: He looks around as if he's waiting for an answer, but he's not of course, the only voice he's really interested in is his own.

I look at our daughter. She screws up her nose as if someone's just shit in her mouth:

[*As* PRINCESS] *Daddy ... I was just playing with my new ball by the fountain ...*

ACTOR 1: Strike one. She's been told the fountain's out of bounds. That's where the rough kids hang out. The poor kids. The ones that sell dope and swig alcohol out of two-litre Coke bottles.

The King's eyebrows start to work up and down and he slides his eyes across at the journalist who pretends not to have heard as she drains another glass of wine.

ACTOR 2/PRINCESS: *... and then, Daddy, it fell into the water and I was too afraid to swim after it ...*

ACTOR 1: Strike two. Last year she pestered and pestered about doing swimming lessons. After three lessons she said she hated it. He shouted and carried on but she's got this way of staring, this sort of 'god, you're so boring' insolent stare. In the end he punished her by shooting one of her ponies.

ACTOR 2/PRINCESS: *... and then, Daddy, this horrible warty frog said that if I feed him at the table and let him sleep on my pillow and be his companion for a week ... he'll get me my ball ...*

ACTOR 1: Strike three. Her father has warts and she knows he's sensitive about them.

And strike four because she can't have a frog sleep with her in that bed. Those sheets are Jacquard-woven, one thousand thread count, Egyptian cotton sateen. From Italy.

ACTOR 2/JEANETTE: I wave at one of the maids and she hurries up to change them to a more serviceable cotton percale.

ACTOR 1/PRINCESS: *... and so, Daddy, I said yes, but I never thought he'd even get out of that fountain, let alone hop all the way here. Daddy, he's disgusting! Can't we just set the dogs onto him?*

ACTOR 2: Her father's complexion has gone deep beetroot purple. The journalist is writing it all down and you can hardly blame her, she can smell a story.

Click click click goes the camera.

ACTOR 1/KING: *You said yes? To the frog?*

ACTOR 2: His eyeballs are bulging from their sockets and he's breaking out in a sweat.

In fact, he's got heart attack written all over him.

[*As* JEANETTE] *Darling ... more fried cheese?*

ACTOR 1/KING: *You're my daughter! A princess! You made a promise! A promise is made to be kept!*

ACTOR 2/JEANETTE: What did he say? A promise is made to be kept! He wouldn't know a promise if it crawled up and bit him on the arse. What about his promise to me?

ACTOR 1: The door opens and we all crane forward to see the Princess's new BFF.

The camera clicks like a possessed beetle and flashes so hard I wouldn't be surprised if epileptics within a five-mile radius are fitting all over the ground.

ACTOR 2: The frog plops in through the door.

ACTOR 1: He's a rather pleasant leaf-green with the usual big boggly eyes.

The Princess stares at the frog, in horror. Mouth curled. Nostrils flared. Pulling back her head like a cobra about to strike.

She doesn't dare leave the table, not after her father's little speech.

The frog hops onto the table with a wet plop.

ACTOR 2: Everyone looks at the frog. And then at the King.

ACTOR 1/KING: *Oh-ho! Welcome! Nice froggy! Good froggy! My castle is your castle.*

ACTOR 2/JEANETTE: The frog ignores him which makes me like it more. It seems to have eyes only for my daughter who is now rolling her tongue back against her bottom front teeth to signify disgust.

Click click click goes the camera.

ACTOR 1: The frog has now edged its way next to her plate and stares up at her without blinking.

ACTOR 2/PRINCESS: *Daddy! Do something!*

ACTOR 1: She looks up at her father wishing the charade would come to an end but he's tearing into his chicken now. Great greasy gobbets of flesh and spittle gathering at the corner of his mouth.

He waves the drumstick at her, the universal signal for: feed the frog.

ACTOR 2/JEANETTE: With a great harrumphy sigh she does, passing it bits of chicken and roast potato. She's careful not to touch it I notice, but it wouldn't be so terrible.

ACTOR 1: The King is smiling contentedly, nodding, as if the frog was always planned, always one big clever publicity stunt.

The Princess has managed to control her rage, turn it inward, face like an angel.

ACTOR 2/JEANETTE: And me … the same.

The camera whirrs and clicks around us.

Journalist closes her notepad. Promises my husband she'll be back. Perhaps a one-on-one? Career trajectory? Wealth accumulation? How he really feels about frogs?

ACTOR 1/KING: *Very good, one-on-one. You'll get a lot more out of me ... heh heh heh ...*

ACTOR 2/JEANETTE: When she leaves, she's forgotten my name, but I'm used to that.

Beat, a look to the audience.

I'm not even in this story.

My husband tells our daughter to take the frog up with her to bed.

ACTOR 1: She stares at him, furious, the camera's gone now, she can't believe he's making her go through with all this. Her darling daddy.

It's so petty, she hisses at him, as she scoops up the frog by one back leg. *Keep your fucking mobile.*

ACTOR 2/JEANETTE: She looks back at me, not scowling, not resentful, and for a moment … She sees me.

Slight pause as JEANETTE *acknowledges this rare moment of recognition.*

ACTOR 1: It will take a week or so. That's what the stories generally say. The frog will be persistent and dogmatic. She will be impatient and appalling. After the fifth day she will feel a change. She will touch his dappled skin and think of dark ponds in deep forests.

ACTOR 2: On the seventh day she will kiss the frog and the real magic will start. They will spend all their time in her bedroom and her father will think she is sulking still.

He will find that amusing.

ACTOR 1: It will be three more days before she admits that the frog has stopped being a frog.

Her father will choke on his roast beef at the thought of her rolling around her virgin bed with her virile prince.

ACTOR 2/JEANETTE: *The servants* will find *that* amusing.

I will be glad I ordered the sheets changed.

And for the first time, I will feel some bittersweet connection with my daughter.

We have both known the magic of love.

ACTOR 1: She kissed a frog and it turned into a prince.

ACTOR 2: I kissed a king and he turned into … an arsehole.

Music: *'Jeanette's Song'*.

SINGER: I saw him standing by the lake
The sunlight in his golden hair
More beauty than a girl could take
His love he said was meant to share

I never thought my heart would break
Like ripples washing on the shore
Marriage was my first mistake
I asked for less, he gave me more

Lights change.

5. HANNAH'S STORY

Transition to city sounds, the wail of sirens, faintly—the smashing of glass ...

ACTOR 2 *brushes at her hair with an old comb as* ACTOR 1 *starts another story.*

ACTOR 1: There once was a big city.

And in that city was a hill.

And on that hill, stood a tower.

Anyone here know the story of … 'Rapunzel'?
Well to us it'll always be …

Slight pause.

The story of … this dear old lady known as … Hannah.

ACTOR 2 *becomes* HANNAH.

ACTOR 2/HANNAH: Like my view?

Look that way and you can actually see mountains. Kid you not. Have a squizz!

Blue sky, sun shining. Bit of forest over there, bit of ocean over there.

It's like the most beautiful cross-stitch you've ever seen. And I've seen some marvelous ones in my time.

They had an exhibition over at the Community Centre and first prize, kid you not, was a three-way tie: Dicky Sampson's 'Weeping Clown', Connie Archer's 'English Cottage with freestyle foxgloves' and Lina up the corridor's 'King [*pronounces it Toot:*] Tut'.

Pause. HANNAH *looks around.*

It's late but. She's not home.

I usually hear her shoes click on the concrete walkway and the screen door bang and the deadlocks go and the door creak.

I can't hear that so I know she's not back.

Not yet.

ACTOR 1: The truth is … Hannah?

ACTOR 2/HANNAH: Fine. We had a bit of a barney. Her and me.

ACTOR 1: Little bit of argy-bargy you could say.

ACTOR 2/HANNAH: Oh I know. It'll all be fine. I'm just a silly old goose.

Hannah, they tell me at the Community Centre, no-one's got in for you, it's just Connie and Dicky and Lina-Up-the-Corridor … they don't have arthritis like you've got, so of course they can get the neat and tiny stitches.

She laughs to herself a little.

Wait, is that her?

She looks up.

No.

Not yet.

We didn't always live here. Her and me. Here, in the Tower.

Started off out in the country. That's it. With a big garden. All the veggies … say a veggie and I grew it. Peas? Got 'em. Broccoli? Yep. Kohlrabi? Certainly did.

Lovely with a bit of white sauce.

ACTOR 1: Her parents lived next door.

Rubbishy little place it was and they didn't do anything to fix it up.

Backyard dead as the moon, completely bare except for a forty-four-gallon drum they had set up in the middle of it. Before she was born.

ACTOR 2/HANNAH: The two of 'em used to fill it with wood and set fire to it and then have parties, loads of teenagers no older than them, standing around the drum with their beer and Jim Beams.

They asked me over a couple of times but I didn't go.

ACTOR 1: She gets pregnant. Has a baby. He starts pinching things.

ACTOR 2/HANNAH: Not a lot at first, couple of apples here and there, tomatoes. Lettuce.

One night I wait on the veranda and when I hear him scrabbling in the dark I flash the torch on him.

Well! Jump? His face goes white as snow.

ACTOR 1/YOUNG FATHER: *Whoa! Whoa! Don't call the cops. Please.*

ACTOR 2/HANNAH: And then he starts babbling on.

About his girlfriend and their baby daughter and the veggies … they gotta have their five and two … and I start to think … this fella's not quite right, you know what I mean?

He's going on about all the voices in his head, first they say: make a salad then they say no, it's got to be coleslaw, then they say no no, ratatouille. And I'm saying alright, calm down, and he's blubbering away saying he'll bring me something in exchange for the lettuce.

I think, fair enough, he might offer to mow the front lawn, but in the morning I open the back door and there's a baby sitting up in a fruit box.

ACTOR 1 *is the baby. She gurgles.*

I mean, *a baby*!

It's ridiculous. But then she starts to cry and so I pick her up. I give her a little cuddle and she stops crying straight away.

Her head smells sweet—honey and milk. I think well, maybe I'll watch her a while.

The baby lies down and goes to sleep.

I don't hear the shots. But I do hear the sirens.

We watch as the police tape around the house but I turn her little face away when they wheel the bodies out.

Came here soon after that. Centrelink, Department of Housing, here. The Tower.

Music.

ACTOR 1: Two bedrooms, galley kitchen and a million-dollar view.

ACTOR 2/HANNAH: Some nights we switch off the telly and just stare across the city.

I brush out her hair till it shines like red silk and she makes up stories about the other buildings or counts the lights or looks for eagles.

ACTOR 1: She starts getting attention from one of the young men on the twelfth floor.

ACTOR 2/HANNAH: *Unwanted* attention, I hasten to add.

Flowers tied to the door handle, that sort of thing. Sometimes he stands in the carpark and calls up her name.

ACTOR 1/YOUNG MAN: *Rapunzel. Rapunzel! Oi! Wotcha up to?*

ACTOR 2/HANNAH: She'll be standing in the window brushing her hair and I'll say: *Get back from the window, pet, you'll fall out, get back!*

ACTOR 1: [*to audience*] You ever hear the sound a body makes when it hits the ground? I always think it sounds like smashing glass.

ACTOR 2/HANNAH: Sometimes she'd ask me to let her go out, walk in the park or get groceries but I say no, you can't do that, not if *he's* roaming about. He could be one of the nutters. Stalkers. Maybe a druggie. Or all three. No.

I keep the door locked and we end up eating quite a few home-delivered pizzas.

And she keeps standing in the window brushing her hair and letting it hang over the windowsill. It looks so beautiful in the sunshine but I tell her: You have to be careful my girl, if that stalker fixates on your beautiful long red hair, you'll be in trouble. Kid you not.

And she says to me:

ACTOR 1/RAPUNZEL: *I'm not your girl.*

ACTOR 2/HANNAH: I knew then. Trouble coming.

One time there's a knock on the door and this voice saying:

ACTOR 1/YOUNG MAN: *Pizza!*

ACTOR 2/HANNAH: Well she goes to open it and I grab her arm, I have a sense about these things and my senses are tingling like a cat in a tumble dryer.

I open the door, just a bit, and when I see the young man waiting on the other side I know. He doesn't have his pizza-place badge on for starters and the other thing is, he doesn't have a pizza!

Go away, I say, *or I'll call the police.* You know what he says?

ACTOR 1/YOUNG MAN: *The police come in their own sweet time, if at all.*

ACTOR 2/HANNAH: I get an idea on how to put him off.

She's watching the telly. I creep up with the scissors and I reach out and …

She pounces on ACTOR 1.

I cut off her hair! It's thick and heavy. I have to hold her down.

She's screaming:

ACTOR 1/RAPUNZEL: *Stop! Stop!*

ACTOR 2/HANNAH: … and I'm shouting: *Hold still! You'll thank me by and by, pet.*

HANNAH *pulls back. The hair is cut. She's panting with the effort. A pause as she looks down at the young woman on the ground.*

You'll thank me.

That sort of cut … it's actually … real flattering on you. Pet.

[*To audience*] She seems angry. With me. Me! Kid you not!

So. Then.

Last night. I wake up
And the door is open—both doors—
and he's standing in front of me.

And I'm terrified. I can't seem to speak.

I think it's a ghost, her father, then I realise … it's him. Her stalker.

Staring at me … like those nutters round here do, in the hallway or in the lifts and then he says:

ACTOR 1/YOUNG MAN: *She's just an old lady.*

ACTOR 2/HANNAH: And I hear *her* say:

ACTOR 1/RAPUNZEL: *She's a witch!*

ACTOR 2/HANNAH: *Watch out, pet! He's a stalker! Don't go near him!*

I wish I had some sort of weapon but all I've got's my cross-stitch needle and thankfully it's largest size on account of my arthritis and I stab him in the leg, I stab and I stab and I stab and I shout:

Get out of our flat! You got no right to be here! Help! Call the police!

And then something slams down on the back of my head and I fall. Right down on the old lino which Department of Housing keeps promising to replace with carpet but never does. And lucky too because getting blood out of carpet's a pig of a job.

She's saying something and my ears are ringing that bad and she gets down on her knees, right next to me to make sure I hear.

ACTOR 1/RAPUNZEL: *You're not my real mother. You can't stop me. Keep out of our fucking way.*

ACTOR 2/HANNAH: He's opened the window. She walks away from me, stands beside him to look over his shoulder.

Slowly, HANNAH *gets up and walks towards the couple standing at the window.*

I'm so close I can hear her say to him:

ACTOR 1/RAPUNZEL: *That's our million-dollar view.*

HANNAH *makes a sudden vicious shoving motion.*

ACTOR 2/HANNAH: I push him hard and he falls over the window and down and then I hear that sound of breaking glass.

She runs. And as she passes me through the doorway, I feel the blindness clawing my eyes, thorns ripping my sight to shreds.

For the rest of my life I will be wandering in the desert with the echo of her voice for company: *You're not my real mother*.

HANNAH *moves blindly back to her chair, listens carefully.*

Hear that?

Sirens in the distance?

She settles herself. Feels for her knitting needles.

I'd like to talk to the police. It can be quite frightening living here, what with all the nutters and druggies and stalkers down below.

There's probably some very nice people about but there's a hell of a lot of bad ones too.

Sirens get louder. Flashing lights of a police car nearby.

Music: *'Hannah's Song'.*

SINGER: On the edge
Take my hand
Steal my heart
Where you can

Catch my breath
From above
Feel this kiss
Fall in love

6. STONE SOUP

Lights change and ACTOR 1 *moves to the soup. It's ready at last. She tastes it and it's beautiful.*

ACTOR 1: Pumpkin soup.

She takes a bowl and carefully ladles some in. She gets a spoon from her hoard and then a thought ... carefully, graciously, brings it to the audience.

She holds it out to someone in the audience.

She waits for them to take the bowl.

She waits for them to taste her soup.

This should be a magical moment. The actor could probably convince an audience member to try the soup. But I think it's important that no words are spoken here.

If there is hesitation, if the audience member is shy or embarrassed or uncomfortable about participating, it becomes even more powerful.

This is about an actor making an offer.

It is also about a character representing all those forgotten characters, making an offer.

The actor is obviously playing that character. She is telling these stories which are both made up and real and structured around other stories that were once also passed on and handed out and shared around people.

Symbolically, a person without power, a home, an income, etc., is presenting a gift to someone who in all likelihood does have all those things.

Sorry, I digress. Back to the stage ...

The audience member accepts the soup . The SINGER *calls out.*

SINGER: Hey, is there enough soup for me too?

ACTOR 2: And me too?

ACTOR 1: Of course there is. Enough soup for both of you. And just one more story.

ACTOR 2: It goes like this:

7. JANE'S STORY

Sound of creaking, things growing, leaves curling.

ACTOR 2: 'Jack and the Beanstalk'.
The story of a woman, Jane.
And her son. Jack.
And this bloody big beanstalk …

ACTOR 1 *is* JANE. JANE *is a recovering heroin addict and a fiercely loving mother. She has a sense of humour and an undying sense of romance.*

ACTOR 1/JANE: It was his dad who had the green thumbs.

If you could have seen the two of them together. Always in the garden, planting things, harvesting things, and the kid digging up worms and trailing chook poo through the hallway. But he was a good boy. Even when they'd stink the place out, I couldn't get mad with either of them.

Not with the kid. And not with *him*. Not with that bloody big grin of his.

Some men have got it all in their smile. The way it lights 'em up. Lights *you* up when they're looking right at you. He'd smile. And I'd smile. And we'd be smiling like a couple of galoots and he'd say something like: *Have a go at this bloody big pumpkin, love.*

And I'd go: *It's bloody big alright.*

And he'd go: *Yep. That's what I call a bloody big pumpkin.*

And we'd laugh like drains and the kid'd laugh too and none of us'd know what the hell was so funny in the first place. But it was.

ACTOR 2: It was good back then.

ACTOR 1/JANE: Back when we had the garden. Me. Him. And the kid. Jack.

Sometimes I look back at the photos and wonder … was that really me, smiling away? Laughing fit to bust like there wasn't a problem in the world we couldn't fix.

Sometimes I wish life was an open book, like they say.

ACTOR 2: A story?

ACTOR 1/JANE: That's it. And if you don't like where it's going, or it gets a bit scary you can just … skip a page.

Jack's dad and me were users. Smackheads. Junkies. It wasn't the whole time but it was a long time.

And sometimes he'd be clean and I'd be using or I'd be clean and he'd be using and poor bloody Jack'd be sent off to my mum's or my sister— the one who's become a born-again.

She said:

ACTOR 2/SISTER: *You should ditch that bloke, Jack's dad. He's a bad influence on the boy. And you.*

ACTOR 1/JANE: I could no more get rid of him than I could … cut off me right arm!

She said:

ACTOR 2/SISTER: I *can't take Jack anymore.*

It's giving you an excuse to get on the gear …

ACTOR 1/JANE: And then she said:

ACTOR 2/SISTER: *It's making it all too easy when you could just make the right choice.*

ACTOR 1/JANE: It's not *easy!*

None of this is easy. I don't *want* to be living like this, from hit to hit. Not enough money to eat properly, to give your kid nice new things, house falling apart, garden full of sticks.

I'm an *addict*, I don't make choices.

You lose all right to choices when you're an addict.

ACTOR 2: Skip a page.

ACTOR 1/JANE: I get clean. And I get a job.

Checkout Chick at first and then they make me Assistant Manager which is about fifty cents better than Checkout Chick but I get a bigger badge. And for a while it's just Jack and me but that's okay.

We see Jack's dad now and then. When he's clean. Now and then.

ACTOR 2: Skip a page.

ACTOR 1/JANE: When Jack was ten, his dad died.

His dad … dropped. An OD. At our place.

Jack and me were out, he came round to see us I guess and was looking round the garden or something. He was found out near the clothes line. The needle still in his arm. He'd shit himself. That happens sometimes.

It was Jack who found him like that.

Flies buzzing around him. Ants in his nose and in his mouth.

Ten years old. What's that for a kid?

I tried to hold it together.

For Jack.

And for me.

I knew I had to be rock solid.

I had DOCS onto me and the school ringing and wanting me to have interviews and my bloody sister in my ear banging on about God's will and bloody work were being complete bastards, not giving me time off to be with Jack. His father and me weren't married and because we weren't living together when he died they reckoned it didn't count. It didn't hurt.

And I just kept taking it. Yep. Sure. No problem. I understand …

But one day, I just crashed and fell and it was so fucking on.

The booze, the drugs, the parties. And I picked up heroin again.

Somewhere around there, Jack started doing the garden.

I told him not to bother: *The ground's shithouse, full of weeds and rocks, nothing good'll ever come out there.*

When he looked up at me, I could have cut the tongue right out of my mouth.

ACTOR 2: And he says: *I've got something.* Holds out his hand. Beans.

ACTOR 1/JANE: *Beans? What bloody use are beans? Least if you get some flowers you brighten the place up …* Stupid. It was like my mouth was connected to my arse or something, fair dinkum, the shit I was sprouting.

All that anger.

All that rage inside of me and now I was spraying it over my little boy.

Our little boy.

Music, gentle, sad.

I loved his dad.

We were more than married. From the first time I saw him, we became tangled in each other's lives. It was as if we grew towards each other, around each other, we gave up sun and rain to be in each others arms. We slept together. Had a child together. Fixed a house together. Dug a garden together.

Got drunk together.

Took drugs together.

Got stoned. Trashed. Hammered. Burned. Fucked. Wasted. Together.

He was my love. My light, my life, my soul. Now he was gone. And I hated him for it.

Music ends.

ACTOR 2: Jack starts disappearing. Starts going out at night and staying out.

ACTOR 1/JANE: *You're too young to be out all night, Jack.*

And he says:

ACTOR 2/JACK: *You were on the nod, Mum. You didn't even know I was gone. You wouldn't give a shit what happened to me. Long as you could get on.*

ACTOR 1/JANE: *No, sweetheart. No. I love you, Jack.*

He just laughs.

ACTOR 2: Skip a page.

ACTOR 1/JANE: Took me six months to kick it that time. Although you're never really safe. I know.

One drink or one shot.

All it takes to send me straight back to hell.

At the end of that six months the Department of Housing tried to evict us for being behind on our rent. And all this time Jack was sneaking around. My good boy. Growing his beans in the backyard. Going out at night. All night.

One night, I catch him.

What have you got there, Jack?

ACTOR 2/JACK: *You spying on me now? It's none of your business, Mum.*

ACTOR 1/JANE: *It is my business if you're dragging something into my house at midnight.*

I can see the bag's heavy. And it jingles.

As I turn on the light, he must have tripped or caught it on a nail or something, because I hear something rip and whatever's in the bag comes tumbling out over the carpet.

ACTOR 2: Gold. Coins. Two-dollar coins actually, thousands of them.

ACTOR 1/JANE: *My God.*

All I could think was … armed hold-up and … sawn-off shotguns and … fifteen years with a ten-year non-parole period and police bashing away on my door to take him away.

Jack! Did you hold up a bank?

ACTOR 2/JACK: *Don't be stupid, Mum.*

Trying to scoop up all the coins and put them back in the bag.

ACTOR 1/JANE: *But you stole it.*

ACTOR 2/JACK: *We need this money. And the guy I took it from has heaps. This'll pay for our rent, Mum. And the food. And the money you owe Aunt Jenny and Gran.*

ACTOR 1/JANE: I dunno what to tell him. I look round the house. It's crap but it's home. Holes in the walls and the taps don't work properly but it's our home and if we took this money we could keep it. We could even find somewhere better. Maybe somewhere with a garden that's still alive.

Jack sees me looking around and he laughs.

ACTOR 2/JACK: *You can even afford to become a junkie again.*

ACTOR 1/JANE: *You have to take it back.*

ACTOR 2/JACK: *Ah, Mum. I was joking.*

ACTOR 1/JANE: *No.* The words are stones in my throat and I spit them out. *Take it back. All of it.*

ACTOR 2/JACK: *But, Mum.*

ACTOR 1/JANE: *You're better than this. We're both better than this. Take it back.*

He was angry. But I knew he'd do what I asked.

He's a good boy.

ACTOR 2: Skip a page.

ACTOR 1/JANE: The next time, he'd stolen a chook.

A bloody big chicken, and the noise it makes at two in the morning as he tries to shove it in his bedroom!

ACTOR 2: Clucking and flapping and him swearing away and trying to shush it—I mean, as if you can shush a chook!

ACTOR 1/JANE: *What are you doing, Jack? We can't keep a chook!*

You need permission from the council, this is an urban area, and what about all the bloody cats around here. Poor thing'll last two seconds outside.

ACTOR 2/JACK: *He's not going outside!*

ACTOR 1/JANE: … Jack tells me.

Well you're not keeping a chook in your bedroom, mate, I can tell you right now.

ACTOR 2/JACK9: *This is no ordinary chook.*

ACTOR 1/JANE: … he tells me and I practically hit the roof.

Well there's NO WAY you're having some sort of foreign chook, Jack! Don't you read the papers? People are dying from bird flu, didn't you know that? This poor thing was probably smuggled in an Indonesian fishing boat.

And by now, the chook's sitting on the carpet with its feet tucked under and its head down. Looking peaky.

ACTOR 2/JACK: *It's not a chook … it's a goose.*

ACTOR 1/JANE: *No, you're the goose! What are you doing bringing a goose home? A sick goose? Listen to the noises the poor thing's making. The police'll be round here wanting to shoot it in the head.*

I go to call WIRES, the rescue people, 'cause I can't stand seeing an animal in distress but he calls me back:

ACTOR 2/JACK: *Mum, look at this.*

ACTOR 1/JANE: He holds something out to me and as I take it, he says:

ACTOR 2/JACK: *This is better than two-dollar coins.*

ACTOR 1/JANE: An egg. But heavy. Much heavier than any egg I'd ever felt. My hand drops and I stagger with the weight of it.

ACTOR 2/JACK: *Look at it. Under the light.*

ACTOR 1/JANE: And I do. It shines, warm and yellow, metallic. And as I bring it closer to my face I see … myself … reflected in gold.

ACTOR 2/JACK: *It* is *gold. This stupid bloody chook lays golden eggs. We're rich, Mum. This is it.*

ACTOR 1/JANE: The egg is warm in my hand.

It's so beautiful, Jack. I've never seen anything as beautiful ...

ACTOR 2/JACK: *I knew you'd like it.*

ACTOR 1/JANE: His face beaming. Lit up. His father's smile.

... but you've got to take it back.

The smile disappears like a star in a stormy sky. He's so angry I think he's gonna hit me. Instead, he starts to cry.

ACTOR 2/JACK: *You're fucking crazy. Fucking junkie. Can't you see I'm doing this for you?*

ACTOR 1/JANE: *I know, love. I know you are. But you've got to stop. They gave me my old job back. And I'm gonna pay all the rent we owe this week. So we'll be okay, Jack. My good boy.*

He snatches the egg from my hand and drags the bird into the room with him.

ACTOR 2: There's a great cackle and ruffle of feathers. He's crying and kicking at the door.

ACTOR 1/JANE: And at one point I hear a smash. I think he threw the egg straight through the glass.

Next morning, very early, I hear him sneak out.

ACTOR 2: He takes the goose with him.

ACTOR 1/JANE: I pretend I'm still asleep.

ACTOR 2: Skip a page.

Last time it happens, he doesn't bother to hide. He comes into the kitchen and puts something on the table. He looks tired and thin and his face is all dirty.

ACTOR 1/JANE: And I just want to hug him and say: it's all right darling. It will be alright. But I don't.

Where have you been? I ask.

ACTOR 2/JACK: *It doesn't matter. I'm busy. Got you this.*

And he walks out of the room leaving me alone. With it.

She uncovers the harp. JANE *stretches out a hand.* SINGER *plays some notes in response.*

ACTOR 1/JANE: Harp.

ACTOR 2: Just a small stringed instrument. Easily tucked between chin and arm.

ACTOR 1/JANE: I can see it's old, like it belongs in a museum, probably worth squillions.

Along one side of the harp is the figure of a naked woman, moulded and curved around the frame.

ACTOR 2: Her arms trail around the edge so that her fingers become lost, tangled amongst the strings and her mouth is flung open as if she is about to sing. Or come.

ACTOR 1/JANE: I pick it up and my hands brush against the strings and as they do, a glorious sound begins to fill the air.

Music begins.

SINGER/HARP: Is this the start
Of something new?
Each moment lasts a year in the magic hour

ACTOR 2: Like sunshine or the golden glow of an egg or a bag of coins, the sound swells and grows and as it does the kitchen seems brighter in response.

ACTOR 1: Brighter, and more beautiful and I know I too am brighter and more beautiful.

SINGER/HARP: I heard your voice
Call out my name
Each breath fills my heart in the magic hour

ACTOR 1/JANE: The sound is better than any high, sweeter than any drug and I close my eyes and drift a little and when I open them again I find myself falling into the arms of Jack's dad who seems to have been waiting all this time for me to hear his call.

The harp sings on and we dance around the kitchen and I'm full of the glow and the sweetness and the light from his smile. That smile. Some men have got it all in their smile.

Lights are beginning to change, sunset, the magic hour approaching.

I can see Jack through the doorway and he's carrying an axe out to the back garden and I worry a little but his dad whirls me round again. [*To* JACK'S DAD] *He's getting so big.*

And Jack's dad says:

ACTOR 2: *Big yes, but never too big for stories.*

ACTOR 1/JANE: And I laugh and say, *How am I meant to get a story round here?*

ACTOR 2: Where there's dry land and dark forests and tall buildings and hardfaced cities, there's always stories …

ACTOR 1: Caught in the gutters and the scary places. In the dry bums of dams and the edges of levees. By the side of the road. And in the backyards of houses just like this one.

[*As* JANE] *Why does he need that axe?*

I ask him.

ACTOR 2: *He's got some pruning to do! Haven't you seen those bloody beans the kid's been growing?*

ACTOR 1/JANE: *I don't go in the garden anymore,* I say. *Not since you carked it out there.*

Jack's dad laughs and we dip.

Well, you should, he says.

ACTOR 2/DAD: *It's taking up most of the garden. Cutting off the light to the houses behind. Stretching up into the clouds.*

The kid's got his giants to kill.

ACTOR 1/JANE: But he's too young for that sort of thing! He's a good kid, I tell him. Our son's a good kid. And suddenly I'm shouting it over and over: *Jack's a good kid! Jack's a good kid!*

Pause.

And then, I'm crying.

And Jack's dad smiles and says: *That's what I call a bloody big beanstalk.*

Music is coming to an end.

ACTOR 2: So they danced, even as the ground shook around them.

ACTOR 1/JANE: Like the book of heaven itself had fallen from God's grasp and lay broken and huge and bloody in the ruins of the back yard.
And when my son came back inside … I washed his face.
I fed him soup.
I said: *I love you.*

ACTOR 2: And they didn't live happily ever after.
None of us did.

SINGER: But we live.

ACTOR 1: Yes. And sometimes,
that's happy enough.

Sunset sky darkening. Music continues as the SINGER *continues. From a garbage bin, curling slowly up into the sky, a beanstalk seems to be growing, tiny lights gleaming and twinkling like stars.*

ACTOR 1: [*slowly*] The hope hour. The love hour. Remembering his touch hour.

ACTOR 2: The fall hour. The small hour. Forgiveness in her call hour.

As the SINGER *plays, the beanstalk reaches the ceiling. Beautiful.*

Other lights appearing, around the bins, curled in and around the rubbish heap.

The space transformed, a blasted heath becoming an enchanted garden.

It is as if the world of the play has been sprinkled with stars.

Magic. The music ends. Silence.

ACTOR 2: The twilight hour.

SINGER: The dreaming hour.

ACTOR 1: The magic hour.

Stars become brighter, and then black.

THE END

THE MAGIC HOUR

BY VANESSA BATES

WRITTEN AND DIRECTED BY VANESSA BATES
PRESENTED BY UPSTAGE AT THE PLAYHOUSE & LULU BELL PRODUCTIONS
CIVIC THEATRE PLAYHOUSE
21 - 30 NOVEMBER 2024

Lulu Bell Productions proudly acknowledges the Awabakal and Worimi people as customary owners of the land on which we work and share our stories. We pay our respects to Elders past and present.

CAST

JAN HUNT ACTOR 1
LOUISE CHAPMAN ACTOR 2
AMY VEE SINGER

CREATIVES

PLAYWRIGHT & DIRECTOR VANESSA BATES
PRODUCER LOUISE CHAPMAN
ART DESIGN STEVE BLACK
COMPOSER & SOUND DESIGNER AMY VEE
ADDITIONAL SOUNDSCAPE ROSS MUELLER
LIGHTING DESIGNER LYNDON BUCKLEY
STAGE MANAGER KATE DUN
OPERATOR ALANA MCGAUGHEY
COSTUME SUPERVISOR KAT HOOD
TECHNICAL SERVICES OPERATOR AMANDA WATT

RUNNING TIME 70 MINUTES NO INTERVAL

REC. AGES 13+ ADULT THEMES

This production was made possible by UpStage at the Playhouse, Civic Theatre, City of Newcastle, thanks to Leonie Wallace and Jordan Campbell. Thanks to Joerg Lehmann Photography. Special thanks to Currency Press.

ABOUT LULU BELL PRODUCTIONS

Lulu Bell Productions' founder Louise Chapman collaborates with writers and directors from Australia, Germany and the United States, creating bespoke solo plays, uncovering stories that are twisted, dark, funny, strange and wise, performed in THE LOU CHAPMAN SHOW and the World Monologue Games. THE MAGIC HOUR is Lulu Bell Productions second collaboration with Vanessa Bates, the first being A REAL THING winning gold at the World Monologues Games 2022.

ABOUT UPSTAGE AT THE PLAYHOUSE

UpStage at the Playhouse is an exciting initiative which has been developed by the Civic Theatre for the City of Newcastle. The program aims to connect with the vibrancy and talent of our local theatre community by co-presenting and supporting works that showcase the ability and creativity of the Newcastle region.

PLAYWRIGHT'S/DIRECTOR'S NOTE

THE MAGIC HOUR was initially written as a solo-performer show, a series of monologues, partly based on fairy tales I had read as a kid in an old, shabby book of *Grimm's Fairy Tales*. Growing up on a diet of Grimm, Blyton, Carroll, Lewis and other amazing books, will do something to a kid. They read. And they write. And some of them grow up and write plays.

For a few years I worked with national arts company Big hART, alongside people living with addictions, violence and poverty. Through theatre and film, working with professional artists, these people's stories were shared with audiences. During this time, I met a lot of amazing women. Mothers, grandmothers, aunties, daughters. All trying to hold a family together, trying to show compassion, trying to understand the drama going on in their family's lives, because often they had experienced it too.

When I sat down to write THE MAGIC HOUR, I thought of these women. I thought of their courage and resilience and their humour. And I knew I could create something that celebrated these stories. But I also wanted something to contain those stories. And that brought me back to fairy tales.

I knew fairy tales were originally part cautionary and part aspirational and quite often dark and just a bit gory. But here's something else I'd noticed. It was to do with the absence of women or at least some women. There was mention of a grandmother here, or a mother there but then often after a brief mention they would prick their finger on a needle and die or, having inspired a prince into action, were never heard from again. Other female characters may have started well but then were simply shelved as "witch". This, then, is the structure of The Magic Hour. Fairy tales retold from the perspective of a missing or sidelined character. A woman.

Re-writing THE MAGIC HOUR for these three performers was exhilarating. As a director, it was wonderful to witness Lou, Jan and Amy creating an atmosphere for storytelling and inhabiting the skins of these characters.

It's kinda simple they seem to say, this play asks you to listen. To the stories that don't make the mainstage. Or the mainstream or the tabloids or the evening news. There is always another story. And we are better people if we can take the time to listen.

I am honoured to acknowledge THE MAGIC HOUR was first written, and then re-written, on Awabakal land. I pay my respects to our first storytellers and to Elders, past, present and future.

VANESSA BATES
PLAYWRIGHT/DIRECTOR

VANESSA BATES
PLAYWRIGHT & DIRECTOR

Award-winning playwright, (Filipino-Australian) Vanessa writes for theatre, television and radio. Ensemble Theatre: THE ONE, LIGHT BEGINS TO FADE. Microtheatre: SMALL HARD TRUTHS. Barking Gecko: A GHOST IN MY SUITCASE. Wyong Art House: TRAILER. Darlinghurst Theatre: EVERY SECOND. Deckchair Theatre: THE MAGIC HOUR Malthouse Theatre: PORN.CAKE. Vitalstatistix: CHECKLIST FOR AN ARMED ROBBER. Sydney Theatre Company: THE BLESSING, DARLING OSCAR. Awards: NSW Premier's Literary Award, AWGIE Award, Inscription Chairman's Award, Inscription New Work Award and the inaugural Stoddart Playwright Award.

Vanessa has been produced by the Sydney Theatre Company, Malthouse Theatre, Barking Gecko, Ensemble, Belvoir B-Sharp, Griffin, Vitalstatistix, Deckchair, Australian Theatre for Young People, Tantrum, Stooged, Freewheels and has written several plays for ABC Radio. Her plays have been performed at the Opera House, Victorian Arts Centre, Newcastle Civic Theatre and the Playhouse. Most works have been published. She is currently a creative practice PhD candidate, writing a television series HALFJAR and researching Mixed Cultural Identity and scriptwriting.

Directing has come rather late to Vanessa. So far, she has directed for Stooged: THE DARK ROOM. Microtheatre: SMALL HARD TRUTHS. Lulu Bell Productions: A REAL THING and Wyong Art House: FLATPACK.
More shall come!

JAN HUNT
ACTOR 1

Jan has performed a diverse range of roles in self-devised, classical and original works with multiple theatre companies. Recent performance highlights include, Newcastle Theatre Company: THE YEAR OF MAGICAL THINKING by Joan Didion (Indie Season). Micro Theatre Festival: SMALL HARD TRUTHS by Vanessa Bates (Janet). WAITING FOR GODOT by Samuel Beckett (Estragon). THE GUINEA PIG YEARS by Vanessa Bates (Narrator, ABC Radio National's Podcast 'FICTIONS')
Awards: Best International Actress, Venice Shorts Film Festival. Best Actress in a Short Film, London Gold Awards (VICTIM) by Jye Currie (Lead Role, Annie). THE MAGIC HOUR gives Jan the opportunity to embrace her passion for storytelling, shapeshifting and sharing other people's points of view, all imbued with a sprinkling of magic.

LOUISE CHAPMAN
ACTOR 2

Civic Theatre Playhouse: THE MAGIC HOUR, CREATIVITY, AWAY, JOYRIDE. Atlantic Acting School: THE WOMEN (Off-Broadway). Sydney Festival: STICKY BRICKS. Commonwealth Games Cultural Festival: SWIMMING THE GLOBE. Sydney Fringe & New Annual: MAD BITCHES, THE LOU CHAPMAN SHOW. Cambodian Space Project: THE ROAD TO TIBOOBURRA. Zenith Theatre: Director CAT ON A HOT TIN ROOF, Assistant Director AFTER MAGRITTE AND THE REEL INSPECTOR HOUND. Perth Fringe & Darlinghurst Theatre: Director THE ANZAC LETTERS. Awards: World Monologue Games: Currently Ranked #1 in the world (Endurance) since 2022. Gold Medal Winner 2022 (A REAL THING), Bronze Medal Winner 2023 (RISE AND FALL OF THE FAIRY QUEEN).

Newcastle Fringe: Best Newcastle Production 2023, Best Performance 2022 (THE LOU CHAPMAN SHOW). Training: Atlantic Acting School New York.

AMY VEE
SINGER

Amy is an award-winning songwriter, performer, and freelance multi-instrumentalist. Amy has toured with Jon English, Tim Freedman, and Sydney musicians' collective The Album Show. Amy is a featured performer on the ARIA-nominated concert film THE ROCK SHOW. Solo, Amy has published four original albums, and supported Newton Faulkner, Luka Bloom, Mark Seymour, and more. Amy's theatre roles include Joan in Stooged Theatre's LOVE SONG and Coral in Pantseat Productions' AWAY (CONDA-nominated). Her long list of music theatre credits includes Very Popular Theatre Company's SUPERSTARS, Svetlana in Very Popular Theatre Company's production of CHESS, and Eva Peron in National Theatre Company's production of EVITA. Amy is psychology graduate and PhD candidate, with published research on the mental wellbeing of professional musicians.

LYNDON BUCKLEY
LIGHTING DESIGNER

Lyndon is an Awabakal/Worimi (Newcastle) based Lighting Designer. He has won several City Of Newcastle Drama Awards. Since leaving Hunter School of Performing Arts, he has worked on many productions across Australia including: Lighting Designer for The Very Popular Theatre Company: MARY POPPINS, JERSEY BOYS, PUFFS, CHESS. HER Productions: LOW LEVEL PANIC. Newcastle Theatre Company: THE EFFECT, A VIEW FROM THE BRIDGE. Newcastle Grammar School: ANASTASIA, WICKED, Bearfoot Theatre Company: TAKE ME TO NEVERLAND,

DO YOUR PARENTS KNOW YOU'RE STRAIGHT. Catapult Choreographic Hub: GRAPPLING AT THE EDGE, AWKWARD, MIXED BILL. LHE Productions: JASPER JONES, AWAY. Associate Lighting Designer for Joshua Robson Productions: LITTLE WOMEN. Crossroads Live: THE ODD COUPLE. Enda Markey Presents: DO YOU HEAR THE PEOPLE SING, BECOMING ELIZA. Make My Mark: HOPELESSLY DEVOTED, TO BARABA WITH LOVE. Darlinghurst Theatre Company: ONCE. Hayes Theatre Company: GODSPELL. Head Electrician and Lighting Programmer for Opera Australia/Sydney Chamber Opera, Belvoir Street Theatre, Darlinghurst Theatre Company and Griffin Theatre Company.

KATE DUN
STAGE MANAGER

After a career that ranges from Landcare to Cultural Development Kate found the creative joy of theatre. In 2010 she produced Newcastle's first Short+Sweet festival before creating Newcastle's Micro Theatre Festival. Micro Theatre produced short plays in coffee shops and art galleries where the venue was the stage. With no mics or lighting this was theatre up close and personal. And it was through Micro Theatre that Kate first met this wonderful bunch of people who now bring you THE MAGIC HOUR. Kate has now moved to stage managing and producing theatre in more traditional spaces. Her nickname is The Ringmaster of Chaos, and her greatest joy is creative teams and projects that help us look at the world anew.

ALANA MCGAUGHEY
OPERATOR

Alana studied Drama Teaching at the University of Newcastle before they demolished the theatre. Her love for theatre has seen her wear many hats in the Newcastle scene, including writing, acting, and directing.

Most recently she directed GRACE UNDER PRESSURE and worked tech for THE YEAR OF MAGICAL THINKING at Newcastle Theatre Company. Alana often thinks about how music and storytelling are so fundamental to our humanity, how we've been doing this for millennia, how ingrained it is within us. Alana is thrilled to be working with both new and familiar faces in this production.

KAT HOOD
COSTUME SUPERVISOR

Kat is delighted to have the opportunity to work with Lulu Bell Productions. An avid theatre lover, Kat has worked at the Civic Theatre Newcastle in a multitude of roles for several years. She works across both the front of house and financial administration departments at the theatre. Kat has assisted on a number of amateur and school productions, as part of the costume team and performing on stage, and is excited to bring that knowledge to THE MAGIC HOUR. She has nearly two decades of experience in sewing and clothing design and can't wait to bring new ideas to life for this performance.

AMANDA WATT
TECHNICAL SERVICES OPERATOR

Loves the people, the space and creativity. Celebrating 21 years at Civic Theatre Newcastle. Highlights include UpStage at the Playhouse: BLUEBERRY PLAY by Ang Collins (Lingua Franca), ROMEO & JULIET: A REIMAGINING (HER Productions). ROCKY HORROR. Seen by over 30 million people worldwide, and performed in over 30 countries, iconic Rock 'N' Roll musical, THE ROCKY HORROR SHOW at Civic Theatre Newcastle starring Australian superstar Jason Donovan as Frank N Furter and Myf Warhurst as the Narrator.